ANCHOR BOOKS

POEMS FOR CHILDREN

Edited by

Neil C Day

First published in Great Britain in 2001 by
ANCHOR BOOKS
Remus House,
Coltsfoot Drive,
Peterborough, PE2 9JX
Telephone (01733) 898102

All Rights Reserved

Copyright Contributors 2001

HB ISBN 1 85930 972 0
SB ISBN 1 85930 977 1

Foreword

Anchor Books is a small press, established in 1992, with the aim of promoting readable poetry to as wide an audience as possible.

We hope to establish an outlet for writers of poetry who may have struggled to see their work in print.

The poems presented here have been selected from many entries. Editing proved to be a difficult task and as the Editor, the final selection was mine.

I trust this selection will delight and please the authors and all those who enjoy reading poetry.

Neil C Day
Editor

CONTENTS

The Blackbird Sings The Blues	Robert Carson	1
The Awkward Child	Ted Harriott	2
Simplicity	Maureen Williams	3
The Suitcase	Marylène Walker	4
Little Bird	Karl Jakobsen	5
The Smallest Angel	Mary Antcliffe	6
Fortescue And Philomena	Mick Nash	7
Teddy	Jennie Pudney	8
The Golden Fleece	Celia G Thomas	9
Delia The Dragon	Peggy Billett	10
Child's Play	Anne Rolfe-Brooker	11
Creeping Crawling?	Anne Macleod	12
The Narrow Boat	Pauline Anderson	13
Pilgrim's Progress	Ivy Cawood	14
On Parade	Margaret Upson	15
Soap In The Bath	Zoe Thomas	16
Nursery Tale	J Cross	17
Bedtime	Zoe Fitzjohn	18
The Magic Cake	Mary Ellis	19
A Little Bull!	Margaret Carl Hibbs	20
The Burger That Never Was	E Wogden	21
Mr Zippy	Emelie Buckner	22
From The Cradle	Ray Ryan	23
A Stranger	J Naylor	24
Sydney The Snail	Doris Moss	26
Jump Man! Jump!	Caroline Tiller	27
Tigger The Terrible	Margaret Bailey	28
Monty Mouse And The Robin	Pam Garner	29
Dinner Plate	Bakewell Burt	30
The Lonely Teddy Bear	Hazell Dennison	31
Two Worlds	R P Scannell	32
Magic Letter	Sarita Wooten	33
Cindy's Fairy Dream	E Kathleen Jones	34

Title	Author	Page
My Mucky Sister	W R Barnham	35
I Always Remember	Mavis Catlow	36
A Daft Poem	John Bracken	37
Whenever You Visit A Dragon	Rebecca Nichol	38
Soil Mates	Geraldine Varey	39
Childhood Summer	Jill Dryden	40
Hoax No Joke	Joyce Clegg	41
The Magic	Joan May Willis	42
There's Nothing There?	Richard Lee Nettleton	43
The Foxglove	Maureen Cassidy	44
A Strange Knock	Mary Buckley	45
Blue Bird's Story	Dawna Mechelle	46
Early Birdie	D E Cornell	47
Brighteyes	Zena	48
The Woolly Mammoth	Irene Snatt	50
UFOs, What Are They?	Christopher Higgins	51
The Goblins	Susan Gordon	52
Tommy Tinker	A L Haskell	53
Growing Up	Betty Green	54
What Am I . . ?	E Langford	55
Simple Cyril	James Kimber	56
Little Green Men	Richard J Bradshaw	57
I Feel Good	Kenneth Mood	58
I Think That My Grandma Is Crazy	Lucy O'Toole	59
Mokey The Lazy Donkey	Annie McKimmie	60
Fairy Land, Fairy Dust	Olive Irwin	61
The Weird Witch	Ray Crutchlow	62
It Wasn't Me, Miss	A-Betty Harrison	63
Best Friends	Sue Hansard	64
Super!	Jonathan Goodwin	65
My Woolly Friend	Majorie H Smith	66
Can You Keep A Secret?	Pat Watson	67
The Little Puff	A R Hawthorn	68
Tick Tack Tavey	Catherine Hislop	69

Uncle Horace	Brian L Porter	70
Little Blackie	Steve Kettlewell	71
Bear	Ted Pyman	72
In Front Of The Looking Glass	Stan Downing	73
Alien Encounter	Trevor Cattell	74
Football Is A Funny Old Game	Tina Rooney	75
What's It Called?	George Main	76
Bubbles	Nigel David Evans	77
Underneath The Stairs	Penny Wright	78
The Witch	Grace Whyte	79
Scamp	John Clarke	80
My Clock	Matthew L Burns	81
Danny Sings	Barbara Williams	82
I Hate	Ann Weavers	83
The Milk Cow	G Bannister	84
A Knight's Tale	Ron Hammond	85
There's A Hole In Your Hair	Y Blake	86
Lottery	W Curran	87
Benjy The Bear	Rachel Harrison	88
Tick-Tock, Bedroom Clock	Pip Hill	89
The Silliest Fairy Tale	H H Steventon	90
The Woods With Robin	Marion Staddon	92
At The Tea Party With Alice	Elaine Harris	93
Snow Martyr	George Pearson	94
Last Word	Liz Sinclair	95
My Kids	Patricia Richards	96
My Girl	Pamela Butcher	97
Kidz	Margaret Grayson	98
Even Bigger Kids!	Paula McKee	99
My Child Dream	Jenny Leyland	100
What To Wear	Lynn Schrale	101
Children	Patricia McGuigan	102
Given Away	Jessica Bartlett	103
The Big Kids	Liam Bates	104
Chameleon	Jennie Atkinson	105

Today's Youth	Julie Grinney	106
IT	Valerie Ramsey	107
James, 13, So Far	D Slade	108
Big Kids On Little Kids	Karen Cormick	110
Big Kids On Kids	Greta Boyd	111
Swiftly Go The Years	Maureen Smith	112
Well Rounded Citizens	S Mullinger	113
The Children	J Wills	114
Little Children	D Begley	116
Growing	Paul O'Boyle	117
Capped Innocence	Leslie Fine	118
Childhood Dreams	A J Renyard	119

THE BLACKBIRD SINGS THE BLUES
(Alice's poem)

O Blackbird what joy you bring,
Your song would wake the dead,
What are those words you 'blithely' sing,
That dragged me from my bed.
The cats were noisy all night through,
The owl tu-whit tu-whooed
And now each morning starts like this,
What can a poor mouse do?
The cats miaul; the owl tu-whits,
The blackbird sings the blues,
The cows are mooing for their lunch,
A dog's now barking too.
The doves are fluttering on the roof,
The thunder rumbles loud -
I wish my ears were very small
And tucked away inside . . .

Robert Carson

THE AWKWARD CHILD

Why do I prefer the wicked witch queen
To the dainty saintly Princess Neat:
Understand the rage of Rumpelstiltskin
Because his noble masters tried to cheat?
Why do I feel pity for the dragon
Slain by greedy men who seek his gold?
Why do I always see another viewpoint
And stretch the teachers' patience sevenfold?
Why do I want to change the definitions,
The rules prepared to sanitise our game?
Why do my schoolmates, in the name of order,
Tell me my doubting brings them only shame?
Why is it wrong to ask that extra question,
Always be the one to raise my hand?
Why does everyone I know avoid me
When all I want to do is understand?

Ted Harriott

SIMPLICITY

When I was a child I couldn't wait,
to see the sea, and buy some chips.
Having a paddle was quite scary
but I really enjoyed these trips.

Back at home we paddled in streams,
my friend John caught some wriggly eels
we walked in the ice cold springs,
until we couldn't feel our heels.

We climbed tall trees and saw a lake
and people fishing there,
the gamekeeper would chase us off,
if we came too near.

From the tree, I thought I saw the Duke and Duchess
they loved shooting and fishing in the lake,
their arrival by majesty car in darkness
gave us much to cogitate.

We walked through woods of bluebells
and gathered hazelnuts,
then we found a shady dell
and made our little huts
of fern and twigs and branches
it really was great fun.

We could hear the pigeons cooing
and sometimes rabbits came,
peeping at us round a tree
as though it was a game.

In the autumn, the sweet chestnuts are ready
and the conkers, collected by boys
to put on strings and have conker fights,
these are such simple joys.

Maureen Williams

The Suitcase

Hiding and purring occupy
Much room and patience
In the suitcase of a cat,

> But a jumper or a sheepskin,
> A dish for cream
> And another for cheese,
> And that's it all ready
> For an outing.

> The next door neighbour's bin
> Soon tempts the cat
> Out of the case,
> The scent of fish bones
> A favourite trail.

> But it's raining a little,
> And it's a cold afternoon,
> And the daylight's somewhat bright,
> So let's get back to the first spot,
> A suitcase left at the airport.

Marylène Walker

LITTLE BIRD

Little bird I saw you hit the high wire in my yard
You've passed it many times before, were you caught off guard?
As you fell and hit the ground, I watched your body lie
My little winter garden friend, I hoped you wouldn't die!
I first see you in autumn eating berries from the ground
A solitary figure among the other birds around
Your red breast can be seen as you move in flight
Darting from tree to tree, like a flash of light!
Just a ball of feathers, with tiny legs and wings
That brightens up the winter days with antics that he brings
Running to the scene below, felt like my heart would burst
With water to revive him and to quench his thirst
But when I reached the very spot, well what more can I say
My little friend had up and left - he had flown away!

Karl Jakobsen

THE SMALLEST ANGEL

The small golden haired girl gazed up at the
beautiful carved Angels in the church roof.
They fascinated her, she longed to touch them.
To run her fingers over their feathery wings.
But they were too high for anyone to reach.

Each Sunday she looked at them during the sermon.
As she and her mother came out of the church each week
there was always an elderly man working on a piece
of wood, behind the font at the back of the church.

He teased her, calling her his 'Little Angel,'
she liked that, because she knew she was no
Angel, her mother often told her so.

The days, months and year passed slowly to the child.
But one bright spring Sunday morning going into
church, to her amazement stood a New Angel
watching over the font.

The man was pleased to see her and said that she
could touch the Angel that he had carved.
Her fingers explored everywhere, the folds of the gown,
the feathery wings, the hands and feet, the locks of hair.
Her small world was complete.

Mary Antcliffe

FORTESCUE AND PHILOMENA

Fortescue and Philomena lived inside a caravan,
In a leisure park quite near the coast,
In the wintertime, they'd sit and shiver in the icy cold
And in the summertime, they'd sit and roast.

They used to spin their little webs and whiz down on a single thread,
They looked like little puppets on a string:
As Fortescue was climbing, Philomena would come whooshing down
And little spider ditties they would sing.

'_ _'
They'd sing as they went spinning round and round
'_ _'
(I don't know how to spell a spider sound!)

Mick Nash

TEDDY

I need to use the bathroom:
I'll always find him there:
He's big and fat and ugly
And covered with black hair.

And when I'm happily bathing
He sits and smiles at me.
He appears to want to join me
But remains there placidly.

I offer him some bubbles:
He smiles and sniffs the air,
I would truly miss him
If he chose not to be there.

And when my bath is over
He is nowhere to be seen.
I guess he's hiding somewhere
To make himself as clean . . .

Jennie Pudney

THE GOLDEN FLEECE

Beneath the stately city walls
Where the shadow of evening falls,
Comes a sound of heavy breathing
With a cataclysmic heaving.

Something moves then with a crash
Rises up in a blinding flash
Of elongated scaly green
With thrashing tail - a monstrous scene.

The eyes are loathsome pools of red,
Bulging out of a serpent's head,
And from the mouth - a crimson gash -
Comes a forked tongue with stinging lash.

As yet no one has found the man
Who can kill this leviathan,
Lying in wait under the oak,
Breathing out deadly fire and smoke.

Jason comes close, but when he sees
The beast his hot blood starts to freeze.
He stands stock still, his muscles lock,
Completely petrified with shock.

Then fate comes to his aid this day
By raising winds that blow away
The fleece which falls into his hand,
As if obeying his command.

But no one else sees this event -
This lucky chance from heaven sent.
So Jason sails back home to Greece,
As champion of the golden fleece.

Celia G Thomas

DELIA THE DRAGON

Delia lets children play on her stomach
It's like a bouncy castle.
When Delia has a sore throat
She gargles with olive oil.
Delia visits her mum once a month
Travelling solo to Timbuktu.
On November the fifth
Delia lights the bonfires.
When Delia runs, beware!
Number five on the Richter scale.
Handy at barbecues
Only eats veggie burgers.
Delia had an uncle called Septimus
He was slain by St George.
When Delia has an itchy back
She has a barbed wire brush to scratch.
Delia has a banjo
She plays tunes for the children.
If you ask Delia to dinner
She loves hot coals and chilli peppers.
Delia lives in a cave on the hill
She loves visitors, just ring her bell.

Peggy Billett

CHILD'S PLAY

There is a place, not far away,
Where gnomes and pixies love to play.
Where trees are made of marzipan
Which if you want to eat, you can.

The lakes are full of lemonade,
And fairies dance within the shade
Of bushes full of cherry drops
And aniseed and Coco Pops.

Marshmallow clouds adorn a sky
Where elephants just love to fly
Above a meadow, made of jam,
Where stands an icing sugar lamb.

Honey vines grow straight and tall,
Their sugared catkins ripe to fall
Upon the grass, which tastes of lime,
Or orange in the wintertime!

Syrup bushes hide small elves,
Who, naturally, just help themselves
To all the jellies they can see
In raspberry and custard trees.

There is a place, not far away,
Where you may go some summer's day.
Where trees are made of marzipan
Which if you want to eat, you can!

Anne Rolfe-Brooker

CREEPING CRAWLING?

A little spider crawling up the wall,
He did but say it all.
A shriek, a scream
He scared my mum
And now he's feeling rather glum.
You see he said
'I'm only really a creeping,
Crawling up the wall.
I really don't mean to frighten at all,
So please will you tell your mum
So I don't need to feel so glum.'

Anne Macleod

THE NARROW BOAT

He glides along the waterways,
Serene in majesty,
The lesser craft hang round him
And gaze in ecstasy.
He does not heed their homage
He proudly passes by
With red and green paint gleaming
His brasses catch the eye.

What cargoes did he carry
So many years ago?
What families did he shelter
Through rain and sun and snow?
Was it coal or was it wood
He carried to the town?
As he manoeuvres through the locks
And carefully slows down.

Big and strong he chugs along
And spreads so wide his wake,
That all the ducks bob up and down
And what a noise they make!
He glides along the waterways
A sight of red and green,
The biggest, brightest, narrow boat
That anyone has seen.

Pauline Anderson

PILGRIM'S PROGRESS

This is the tale of a slow-moving snail
Who lived round our garden shed.
His name was Ben, an' he made a den
So cosy and warm for his bed.

He knew it was risky if he got too frisky
And strayed a long way from home.
But then he got bold, and wouldn't be told,
An' that's when he lost his foothold -

He slipped and fell, into a bluebell;
Who was shocked and knocked down low.
'Ugh, what's the matter? - You can just scatter!
You've given me such a blow!'

So back he went, for he wasn't meant
To live so far away . . .
But on a turn he met a worm
As slow as him; just as lost - anyway.

They kept together, then a change in the weather
Brought rain to add to their woe.
But Ben had his umbrella, not like the worm (poor fella!)
So come on it's not far to go . . .

At last they reached home,
Oh; no more will I roam!
(With feet like lead) 'I'm going off to bed!'
'So am I,' said the worm - 'I'm half dead.' 'Nuff sed.

Ivy Cawood

ON PARADE

Right said Sergeant Ben, carrying his cane,
We'll march up the hill and back again.
Today the soldiers were on parade,
The regiment band was being played.

The camp was put under guard,
All visitors today where barred.
No one could go into the town,
They all had a good dressing down.

All the barracks scrubbed and shone,
No one seemed to know what was going on.
All the soldiers were in uniform,
Parading around from early morn.

Out of a plane dropped a parachute,
A parachutist was a box, dressed in a suit.
When they all got over the shock,
It was the new mascot with a white sock.

To them it was royalty by itself,
Like the photo on the major's shelf.
To the company it was a relieve
After it settled, some went on leave.

Margaret Upson

SOAP IN THE BATH

It slips and slides
It jumps and dives
Then at the bottom
Of the bath it hides.
It lurks at the bottom of the bath
And I have to follow its path.
Then comes the bit I hate,
When it starts to disintegrate!
So I have to get out quick
And out of the bath
My soap I pick.
It acts in a most disobedient way
That's why my soap
Gets thinner each day!

Zoe Thomas

NURSERY TALE

Sleeping Beauty fell asleep,
Little Bo Peep lost her sheep.
Humpty Dumpty had a great fall,
Cinderella went to the ball.

London Bridge is falling down,
Jack fell down and broke his crown.
Pussy Cat frightens a mouse under a chair,
Johnny's so long at the fair.

Mary, Mary's garden is in bloom,
The cow jumped over the moon.
The little dog broke out in laughter,
They all lived happily ever after.

J Cross

BEDTIME

Lay your sweet head down upon your bed,
Think of your day and what lies ahead.
Dreams I hope are happy and sweet,
All night long please don't peep!
A kiss I place softly on your face,
Gently stroking your hair back in place.
When tomorrow comes it shall be a new day,
Now that's all I must say,
Sleep tight, goodnight.

Zoe Fitzjohn

THE MAGIC CAKE

One day a baker began to bake
A very special kind of cake.
He baked it at the midnight hour
After making it with Fairy Flour,
Which was made for him in Fairyland,
And quite untouched by human hand.

He iced the cake in white and gold,
And it was very quickly sold
To a rich king who came by
To order a large peacock pie,
Because he was very fat and greedy,
And never gave to the poor and needy.

He showed the cake to his wife,
Who sliced it with a diamond knife.
She said, 'It does look rather nice,'
But he didn't give her a single slice.
He just ate up every crumb,
And said 'That was good, by gum!'

But later he moaned, 'I do feel queer'
And then in a mirror hanging near
He saw he was now *a big fat pig*.
In his rage he danced a frantic jig,
But the queen just said with a sigh,
'Take this pig out to a royal sty,
He won't need a crown anymore
We'll sell it and give a feast to the poor!'

Mary Ellis

A LITTLE BULL!

A jolly Hippopotamus
Said, 'This is very ominous,
A little Bull adorable
Has caught a cold incurable.
Bless my soul! What shall we do
If treatment's not available?'

'Fear not!' exclaimed a Nonny-Mouse,
'Take him to a coffee house,
And get some toddy hot enough
To cure his beastly tickly cough.'
'Oh, that sounds very sensible,'
Said Hippo: 'Most commendable.'

But crafty greedy Crocodile
Said, 'This is inexcusable,
I'll cure our little Bully Bull
Of ailments quite invincible.'

But thoughts of saucy Crocodile
Snapping at his valuables,
Made Bully, who's excitable
And clearly *not* expendable,
Snort - 'This is quite intolerable!'
And charge with all his might.

The moral of this story is:
Don't inflame a Bull!

Margaret Carl Hibbs

THE BURGER THAT NEVER WAS

The sausage and the teacake met at the celery tree
And teacake said to sausage 'Do you belong to me?'
Now sausage thought a little while and then replied 'What's up?'
'We can't belong together, we have no red ketchup.'
So off they went together to find this very sauce.
Now this is where this poem ends, I'll tell you why because,
They came across a hungry boy whose name was Greedy Bill.
Before they knew what happened
Greedy Bill had had his fill.

E Wogden

Mr Zippy

Mr Zippy is in town,
Mr Zippy, the famous clown,
His face is painted yellow and red,
A purple parrot sits on his head.

Mr Zippy's eyes are green,
He's the tallest clown you've ever seen,
His legs are so long! His feet so big!
His boots are brown boxes, his hair a white wig.

Mr Zippy wiggles his ears,
Walks on his hands, cries buckets of tears,
He takes giant footsteps, falls into a hole,
Slithers and slides down a long greasy pole.

Mr Zippy laughs a lot,
On the end of his nose is a bright blue spot,
He presses a button on his chest,
And a fountain of water spurts out of his vest.

The children laugh, the children scream,
He's the funniest clown they've ever seen.
Today the circus tent came down,
Mr Zippy is leaving town.

Mr Zippy has gone away,
He said he'd come back another day.

Emelie Buckner

FROM THE CRADLE

Thank you daddy and mummy for letting me be born
Life so far is very good, for me it's early dawn
I heard some sounds, I saw some light
Sleep and feed were my delight.

I felt your warmth when you cuddled me
Sure but slow I began to see
Shapes and sounds, the fun of games
Colours bright with yet no names.

I'm learning now to play with toys
The pure delight of making noise
I've found my hands and little toes
My mouth and eyes and stubby nose.

Food and sleep are still the best
But I'll quickly learn the rest
Soon I'll find out how to crawl
Then I'll really have a ball.

In my time I've come to know
Your voices, faces and the love you show
Mummy, daddy, I will try to be
As near to good as is really me.

Ray Ryan

A Stranger

One day I sat in the park
No one was there but me,
Suddenly there was a noise
I turned around to see,
A strange looking creature
He looked like a cube,
Had long furry floppy ears
Nose shaped like a tube,
Green eyes with bright yellow rings
No mouth that I could see,
Had these wiggly, squiggle bits
Which were, pointing at me,
One on each corner of his head
They motioned me to follow,
To a tall tree standing there
Its trunk dark and hollow,
We whizzed high, into the air
Through white clouds in the sky,
Stop at this, big black hole
Thought I was going to die,
Creatures of many forms
Could not believe they're seeing,
A thing from another place
Had never seen, a human being,
Became very friendly
We did all sorts of things,
Had a meal of squiggle bits
Pudding, red shape with wings,
Saw square worms and odd insects
Red snakes with stripes of blue,
They were triangle shaped
It's true, I swear to you.

I will remember these odd things
If ever I get home,
I think I will avoid the park
Not far will I roam.

J Naylor

SYDNEY THE SNAIL

Sydney the snail leaves a long silver trail
As he glides through Gran's garden at night.
He slithers around without making a sound
As he eats all the green leaves in sight.

My gran gets annoyed
All the flowers are destroyed, as he munches
Great holes in the leaves
It costs lots of money
But is really quite funny
As she buys yet six more packs of seeds.

Gran cries 'Sydney the snail I'll put salt on your tail
If you don't stop this nonsense for sure,'
And perhaps Sydney heard
Though it seems quite absurd
But he comes to Gran's garden no more!

Doris Moss

JUMP MAN! JUMP!

'I'm afraid you'll have to jump'
Scoffed the camel with one hump
'Am I supposed to perch on there?'
The goaded man wailed in despair.

For having hired the one-humped breed
The Arabian noted for its speed
He now stared at its awesome mound
A good few feet off solid ground.

The Bactrian boasts a two-humped seat
And are for riding quite elite
For all a learner has to do
Is wedge themselves between the two.

But this man with his foolish pride
Insisted on his pre-paid ride
And hoped to jump upon his seat
By tying springs beneath his feet.

The camel thought it was a game
Until he bounced with deadly aim
Alas, it then recoiled in fright
And so the target sank in height.

Then skyward the poor rider flew
Until he disappeared from view
And finally there came a yell
That echoed from the village well.

Caroline Tiller

TIGGER THE TERRIBLE

I have a naughty Scot called Tigger,
Thank goodness he will get no bigger!
Named for the bouncy friend of Pooh
He started off when nearly new.
When still a pup he chewed his bed,
Lino and several balls instead
Of his nice dish of Pedigree Chum,
Much better for his poor old tum.
But he preferred some sticky plaster,
A feat that ended in disaster!
A hasty trip to see the vet
The plaster round his paws had set.
His next exploit was very bad
He chewed up all the post I had!
When he barks the neighbours say,
'I wish that dog would go away.'
He understands me when I talk
Especially if I mention 'walk'.
There is one word he fails to know
The short but simple word is 'No!'
He is a hellhound though so small
But I adore him, warts and all!

Margaret Bailey

MONTY MOUSE AND THE ROBIN

Monty Mouse lived in a house
Under an old tree in a wood.
He often did the things he shouldn't
And not the things he should!
One day he thought he'd run away
To see the world outside.
He put some cake crumbs in his pocket
And a slice of apple pie.
He crept across the meadow
And then he got afraid
He didn't like the big black crow
That sat upon a tree.
He didn't like the buzzing of a great big bumblebee.
He turned for home to find his Mum
But didn't know the way.
'I'm lost' he sobbed 'I'll never find
My little house again.'
A little robin hopped to him
And said 'You've left a trail of cake crumbs
Which I am going to eat
But if you follow me
I'll take you to your little house
Underneath the tree.'
That's what they did and Monty said
'Robin I'm so glad you found my trail of crumbs
Do call any time you're free
And stay and have a piece of cake
And a cup of mousy tea.'

Pam Garner

DINNER PLATE

'Come on -mush - make us some room'
Said the toadstool, on the plate
About to be eaten
To the steak, about to be - too.

Once I enjoyed life,
Hidden amongst the grass in a field,
'And I used to eat it'
Said the steak, 'For a meal.'

But look where it's got us,
We're both in the same boat
And this time it's our turn,
Let's hope they all choke!
Because when you're the one being eaten,
Well! - Really it's no joke!

Bakewell Burt

THE LONELY TEDDY BEAR

The lonely teddy bear sat in the toy shop all alone,
He really wasn't happy, sat there with a frown
Little girls and boys had held him but put him back again,
Could he find someone to love him and take away his pain?

Next day a little girl came up to him,
He gave her such a cheeky grin,
'I'd love to take you home with me' she said
'Mummy will tell us lots of stories when we go to bed.'

Mummy replied 'You can have the teddy for your birthday dear,'
So from now on the teddy had nothing to fear.
With hugs and kisses he felt so grand,
He was the happiest teddy bear in all the land.

Hazell Dennison

Two Worlds

My little friends, hold my hands, together now, we walk
Into a wonderland, we now have wings, we are flying
With the birds, then rest a while, in tops of trees,
In our wonderland, we are driving a steam train, on its way
To the seaside, a place we stop, to build our castles out of sand,
Then surrounded by a moat, to keep the coming sea at bay,
More delights, we are in a jungle wild and free.
There are animals all around, each one we call by name,
Now we must make our return, to the other world,
As we hear a call from Mother dear, your tea is ready now.

R P Scannell

MAGIC LETTER

If you believe in your heart,
About fairies and dragons.
Then it's true,
If it makes you happy to believe
All kinds of magic,
The magic will stay with you forever.
It makes a child like you,
Imaginative, hopeful and good,
Thoughtful and kind.

Throw away the wicked goblins,
There's no such people,
Only kind goblins and fairies
That you will find.
In the best picture books
And in kind people,
Who will help you.

There's a castle and palace
For each boy and girl.
There's magic in everything good,
It doesn't have to be glitter or gold,
Just nice thoughts and plans.
Then you'll have the magic of the land.

Always believe in goodness,
You'll always have a friend,
Always believe this is true.

Magic is built from nothing
Then it turns to something,
No matter how long it takes,
It will be there.

Sarita Wooten

CINDY'S FAIRY DREAM

Lindy was a little girl with wonderful imagination,
I can verify that without any hesitation,
Fairies and pixies were her favourite delight,
Sure that if only she could be out late at night,
She would see them in the garden by the light of the moon,
Dancing around to a fairy-like tune.
So one warm summer's eve, she got out of bed,
And by the light of the moon, able to tread.
The well used path to the seat by garden wall,
Sheltered by branches of the oak tree tall,
Suddenly the sight that met her astounded view,
Were elfin figures, dancing in line, two by two,
The fairies were arrayed in white gauzy dresses,
Jewels adorning their person and hair tresses.
Pixies with pointed hats and tunics of green,
Altogether making an enchanting and idyllic scene.
Then the fairy queen wearing a floral crown,
Came to Cindy, taking her hand and leading down,
To join in the fun, as she happily danced around.
Her feet barely seeming to touch the ground.
Suddenly the moon was hidden and she felt herself quiver,
She opened her eyes, beginning to shiver,
Evening mists shrouding all from view,
Where were the fairies, and pixies too?
She glanced around with rising agitation,
Surely it hadn't all been her imagination,
It had been too real, so vivid and clear,
But she had to admit it did appear,
She could have fallen asleep, and dreamt it all,
But something she'd always remember and with pleasure recall.

E Kathleen Jones

My Mucky Sister

I've got a younger sister who is a real mucky miss,
To play with mud and water for her is sheer bliss.
She can't stay clean a minute not that she really tries,
As soon as Mum turns her back she's making more mud pies

If she is dressed in her Sunday best when going out somewhere,
Until we are ready to leave the house we tie her to a chair.
Or else she'd find some water and mud to drive my mum insane,
Then we'd have to hose her down and start all over again.

When she is older - she just can't wait to grow,
Her great desire is to go on a TV show.
Where you sit in a tank and in a very short time
You are then deluged in a gooey green slime.

W R Barnham

I Always Remember

Trees shaded the bluebells
Oh! Those happy days,
Out with my parents
Beneath the sunshine's rays.

Looking back to those moments
Filled with so much fun,
And I always gave my parents
Nature's bouquet of flowers
When day was done.

Mavis Catlow

A Daft Poem

The Slumgullions and Slimgallions
Were mortal foes.
They fought through the centuries,
As history shows.
Why all the fighting?
Well! Nobody knows,
The Slumgullions had pink feet
Without any toes.
The Slumgallions had no feet,
But grew toes on their nose.
Was this why they fought?
We'll never know.
For they all died out,
A long time ago.

John Bracken

WHENEVER YOU VISIT A DRAGON

Whenever you visit a dragon,
Whether it's sneezing or not,
Approach on your toes and keep clear of its nose,
For a dragon sneeze tends to be hot.

Whenever you visit a dragon,
If smoke issues forth from its lair,
Do not go inside or you're sure to be fried -
If it suffers from chills then beware!

Whenever you visit a dragon,
You must always take it some food,
Or it'll eat you without having to chew
And find you remarkably good.

Whenever you visit a dragon,
Be sure to stay very polite,
Else it will blow hard and you'll return charred
And give your relations a fright.

Whenever you visit a dragon
(I assure you that dragons are real)
Just keep these few rules and, unlike some fools,
You're its best mate and not its next meal!

Rebecca Nichol

SOIL MATES

He's playing with the worms again,
He thinks that they can fly,
He holds them high above his head
And points them to the sky.
He makes a funny buzzing sound
Whilst leaping up and down
He's oh so disappointed though
When they come crashing down.

They are his special playmates
He loves their funny ways,
They never let him down at all
And never tell bad tales.
Sometimes they play hide and seek
And disappear for days.
Then somehow quite by magic
They come out to see the rain.

He knows that they like water,
He pours it on the soil
And then he waits and laughs with glee
When they all come to call.
He wishes he could be like them
And live under the ground
He doesn't really like his house
On the edge of town.

Some day he'll have a tiny place
With lots of soil behind.
He'll sit with all his wriggly friends
And have a lovely life.
His dreams will all come true at last.
Why can't I be that boy?

Geraldine Varey

CHILDHOOD SUMMER

When the sun does shine
And the sky is blue
The world takes on a different hue
Holidays start for one and all
The cases are packed with pail and ball

To the seaside we go full of glee
We know we'll only be in for tea
Our faces are brown, our legs are too
We always find plenty to do.

The days are long with nice long nights
We can sit outside without any lights
When our holiday ends, in our eye there's a tear
We'll now count the days till our holiday next year.

Jill Dryden

Hoax No Joke

All you little kids out there,
When you dial the brigade, 999,
You could be putting someone's life,
Right there on the line.
Someone else might need them,
While they're answering your hoax,
It might be a tiny baby,
- Or maybe some old folks.
So before you dial that number,
- Before you make that call,
It may be one of your family in need,
- It might even be them all.

Joyce Clegg

THE MAGIC

As we climbed aboard
The wooden box
Our John, Michael, Teddy and me
That won't fly! They all shouted with glee.

But we knew the words
Full of magic you know
That would make out
Flying machine go.

We said our goodbyes
Then off we went
We circled and swooped
Oh! What an event.

They came to the windows
To wave us goodbye
Then over the playground
We went with a cry.

Then we flew through the sky
Leaving sparks as we went
And the moon as it rose
Gave us light to descend.

We chattered and laughed
As we landed at home
And told of the fun
That we'd had at Toytown.

We'd go there again
Sometime when it's right
We murmured to Mum
As she tucked us up tight.

Sometime! When the magic is right
Then again we can fly through the night.

Joan May Willis

There's Nothing There?

Last night, and through my inner ear.
I sat to listen, but could not hear,
That sound, a noise which through each night,
Had scared and filled me full of fright!

Did I hear, or did I miss,
The lowly rumble, the silent hiss?
That serpent, entangled in my brain.
And now I lay here once again!

My eyes grow weary, there's nothing there
But the black of darkness, yet do they care?
Those evil terrors have come again,
To haunt and taunt and cause me pain.

It's there once more! I strain to hear,
Then shout out loud, 'You're not out there'
Hoping against hope they'll go away,
And knowing they will, come the light of day.

But as I lay quaking, tucked up here in bed,
Could these be the calls from those now long dead?
Then I strain my ears to hear that sound,
The one that's not there, yet all around.

Richard Lee Nettleton

THE FOXGLOVE

Its freckled flowers of brightest pink
Play host to bumble bees who come to drink
Quickly the bees fly, deep down inside
Such a snug fit, with nowhere to hide
Staying for a moment, then away they fly
Until they are just a small speck in the sky.

Foxglove flowers fall to the ground
Lying there till by the pixies found
Pixies sell them, or so I've been told
To foxes for lots of bright shiny gold
They sew them into the finest of gloves
That vain foxes, wear for their lady loves.

If you venture out on a moonlit night
You could be a witness to a wonderful sight
As a pixie creeps from beneath furry leaves
Darting upwards on spires so nimbly he weaves
And in that merry way he cheerily assumes
Plucks one of the foxgloves, sweetest blooms.

Waving the flower aloft in his hand
He holds a hat, so perfect and grand
Excitedly he pulls on his coat of crimson red
And places his new hat onto his tiny head
So, if in the night you hear the strangest shout
Don't worry it's just a happy pixie gadding about.

Maureen Cassidy

A Strange Knock

Nonnie from nowhere knocked late on my door.
I looked out but Nonnie was nowhere about.
I searched there but Nonnie was not to be found.
I went in but then, the knock came again!
That's Nonnie from nowhere. Where is she? I said -
I peeped out but Nonnie was nowhere. Oh then!
Why does Nonnie from nowhere knock late on my door?
Where is Nonnie from nowhere? Is she somewhere around?
Who is Nonnie from nowhere? Is she a coward?
When I go in, oh then, why! She knocks me again.
It's time Nonnie from nowhere got tired of her game
Go home Nonnie from nowhere.
Your Mother's going spare.
You're a pest!
    Have a rest!

Mary Buckley

BLUE BIRD'S STORY

Bluebird was merrily skipping home,
When she bumped into Hodgey the hedgehog,
'You look happy' he said.
'Mouse asked me on a date, to dinner' Blue Bird said.
'Fantastic' he said.
And off she skipped,

When she saw Olive the rabbit,
'Why, you look happy' she said.
'Mouse asked me on a date to dinner,
And gave me a beautiful rose' Blue Bird said.
'Fantastic' she said.
And off she skipped,

When Frances the frog called her,
'Blue Bird, you look happy' she said.
'Mouse asked me on a date to dinner,
Gave me a beautiful flower and then kissed me' Blue Bird said.
'Fantastic' she said.
And off she skipped,

When she saw cat,
'Cat' she called.
But cat was not listening,
'Cat, Mouse asked me for a date to dinner,
Gave me a beautiful flower and a kiss' Blue bird said.
'Oh nice' said Cat.
As he licked his lips,
Smiled a satisfying smile,
And lazily walked away.
And off Blue Bird skipped,
To get ready for her dinner date.

Dawna Mechelle

Early Birdie

A robin did a plan devise
On how to make an earthworm rise
From his home within the ground
Fat and juicy, plump and round

He thought he'd charm it like a snake
With a tuneful song that he'd make
Then he'd grab it in his beak
So that juicy worm couldn't make a squeak.

Well, all was fine and the earthworm rose
From his home in which he dozed
He danced and swayed to the robin's song
But all at once his plan went wrong
For as the robin stopped his tune
The earthworm slid back in his home
For the trance would cease when the music stopped
And back in the ground the earthworm popped.

Poor robin sang and sang all day
In an effort to catch his slippery prey
But in the end with nothing to eat
He had to admit defeat
The earthworm he'd had the greatest fun
Dancing all day in the summer sun
And poor old robin it is true
The earthworm made a cuckoo of you.

D E Cornell

BRIGHTEYES

Just three feet from my sunroom
roses, plants and flowers abound,
Plus, a little rabbit - plants and shrubs
are edible she's found.

Every day she comes a digging,
looking for different things to eat,
She knows she can rely on me, to fill in
and having it looking neat.

To my surprise, she's giving birth -
five off-springs hidden in the hollow
She does a very clever job shoring up,
then she calls, I'll be back tomorrow.

Early every morning she comes - and
instantly they know she's there,
She removes a little soil and they're
there jostling for their share.

It's the tenth day now, she comes to feed
and tend her happy brood
No cover-up this time, she leaves
the entrance open to be viewed.

I'll keep watch, I'll see they're safe -
from all those cats next door,
I couldn't bear her to return
and find she's only four.

It's day thirteen she leads them out,
but soon they're back to the safety of the burrow,
It's a big world out there my loves,
it will be all yours tomorrow.

The garden seems quite empty, Brighteyes
and her family have fled,
It's back to watching the birds and bees
and the butterflies, instead.

Zena

THE WOOLLY MAMMOTH

There was a woolly mammoth,
Henry was his name.
He was so very clumsy
That he often blushed with shame.

At dinner with the Mastodons
He got in such a state.
He dropped his knife
And soon his cup
And then he broke his plate.

Mrs Mastodon was cross.
'You've broken my best service.
It belonged to dear Mama.
O what a dreadful, clumsy,
Useless animal you are!'

Henry went home sadly
And hid within a cave.
He could not eat,
Would not go out
And did not want to shave.
It's thought he died of hunger
And there his bones have lain
Ten thousand years in slumber -
Now they've dug him up again.

Irene Snatt

UFOs, What Are They?

UFOs, what are they? Where are they from?
One moment they are there, then they are gone,
How do they get here? How on Earth do they fly?
Forever appearing and vanishing in our sky,
Unidentified Flying Objects or just UFOs,
Do they exist? Are aliens here? No one knows,
Are they in our imagination? Or possibly real?
Is this part of their common religious appeal?
Could alien abductions and Men In Black be true?
A solution to this psychological mystery is due,
Are these empyrean visitors friends or foes?
When they are finished here, where do they go?
Flying saucers and UFOs in many shapes and sizes,
Are they extra terrestrial or non-existent devices,
Are UFOs normal aircraft, or a mistake, unaccused?
With aliens, ETs, or whatever label you want to use,
Can the most exciting date in our history be far away,
When we meet our cosmic neighbours on World Contact Day.

Christopher Higgins

THE GOBLINS

Goblins live in the forest so green
And although they are difficult to be seen
They're the grass on the ground, they're the leaves on a tree
Look very closely, a goblin you'll see.
Some goblins are bad, some goblins are good,
Some make you happy, some steal your food.
They tickle your nose, your ears, your knees
And they know itchy noses will make you sneeze.
And when you sneeze, a baby goblin is born
In the quiet and stillness of a forest dawn.

Susan Gordon

Tommy Tinker

Little Tommy Tinker tumbles all about;
Look at Tommy dancing, the other children shout.
Little Tommy Tinker thinks that he'll go far,
With his pirouettes and cartwheels, he thinks he'll be a star.

But little Tommy Tinker will not learn to read or write;
He keeps showing off and prancing, morning, noon and night.
Little Tommy Tinker, thinks he'll be rich and famous,
But if he doesn't soon behave, he'll be just an ignoramus.

A L Haskell

GROWING UP

You wonder why the grown-ups treat you as if you don't know,
Don't worry it's for your own good you'll learn that as you grow.
Some days you look so woe-be-gone
And you're wrong in all you've been and gone and done.
You little face tells it all,
But Mummy and Daddy don't want you to fall.
When things all seem to be going wrong,
Why not hum a little song.
Try to wear that sunny smile,
It will help you all the while.
You can be such a happy soul,
But others will only play when you are whole.

Betty Green

WHAT AM I..?

Helicopters flying things
helicopters lateral wings
flying lower than its namesake
flying higher than the wind break.

Built for one flat on his back
or twenty very short and fat
landing on the airport pond
of reed beds we are very fond.

Flying only summer days
along side other wings ablaze
have no need to call the tower
land on any leafy bower.

Take off takes a mini second
and then when pollination beckons
latest technological compass
change direction cause no rumpus.

Have no need of noise abatement
never hear from house complainant
silent engines, natural fuel
maintenance free, annual renewal

Accidents never occurring
a summer breeze is what is stirring
I know you don't give but a damn
you'll know by now though
who I am . . .

E Langford

SIMPLE CYRIL

Simple Cyril met a squirrel
whilst going to the fair,
said Simple Cyril to the squirrel,
'What will you do there?'

Squirrel was a fortune-teller,
and once inside his booth
he'd tell a tale to make you wail,
but seldom told the truth.

He promised futures very bright,
with money soon in view;
and everybody paid and smiled,
seemed they believed it true!

Simple Cyril from the Wirral
learned something that day;
few people ever tell the truth,
because it doesn't pay.

James Kimber

LITTLE GREEN MEN

There are little green men living in my garden.
I have seen them from my window just at dawn.
Gaily standing on their heads
In the furthest flower-beds,
Or turning merry cart-wheels on the lawn.

There are little green men living in my garden,
Always having fun and never sent to schools.
Chasing round the apple tree,
How I wish that one was me,
Not controlled by silly grown-ups, and their rules.

There are little green men living in my garden,
And their homes I cannot find, although I try,
So perhaps they go to bed
Snug inside our garden shed,
For that's the only place to keep them dry.

There are little green men living in my garden
And the only work I've ever seen them do
Is to spend the sunshine hours
Painting all our garden flowers.
My mum just says I'm lying, but it's true.

There are little green men living in my garden,
But my dad says such strange beings cannot be,
So I ask them in to play,
But they always run away.
Oh! Why can't grown-ups see them, just like me?

There are little green men living in my garden
Where they get involved in many pranks and tricks,
But when older folk come near
Strange to say, they disappear,
For adults and little green men do not mix.

Richard J Bradshaw

I Feel Good

Sometimes we get ourselves all mixed up
The stress and the tension take control
But with a little thought
We can rise above it all
Float away to another place -
A holiday dream or a lottery win.

Sometimes we get trapped in the material world
And make ourselves depressed,
It's best to relax and look at the funny side
Go on, try and laugh now
Make yourself laugh each hour in the day
Your health will improve, I guarantee.

Kenneth Mood

I Think That My Grandma Is Crazy

My grandma is strange, her sentences rhyme
But we all think her highly amusing
'I've taken up sailing, the banshees are wailing'
You see what I mean, she's confusing.

'My gums have been itching, I think it's all the stitching
My jaw is now coming apart
My stomach is rumbling, the food is all tumbling
And out from the back comes a fart.'

'The goldfish have fleas, my legs have no knees
The milkman delivers the post
Badgers are bold, the oven is cold
Does that mean I can't cook the roast.'

'Ferrets wear stilts, the Irish in kilts
Poodles have silky straight hair
Squirrels in knickers, monkey nose pickers
The boy ran away with the fair.'

'Werewolves love shaving, baths aren't for bathing
Just to lie back and be lazy
A witch with no spells, the church lost its bells
I think that my grandma is crazy.'

Lucy O'Toole

MOKEY THE LAZY DONKEY

He was a lazy donkey,
Who wouldn't move an inch,
I pulled him and I pushed him,
But he didn't even flinch.

For he just stood and laughed at me,
Hee! Haw! Hee! Haw! He said,
You'll never make me move from here,
I simply won't be led.

Then I had a brilliant notion,
I found a piece of stick,
Attached it to a carrot,
With string, that did the trick.

I dangled it in front of him,
Hee! Haw! Hee! Haw! He said,
Now that's a juicy offering,
As up the road we fled!

Now Mokey was a silly ass!
He was a stupid Ned!
He thought that he could laugh at me,
But I hee-hawed instead!

Annie McKimmie

Fairy Land, Fairy Dust

There is a place call Fairy Land
where the fairies live.
Where children's dreams go.
Where there is wild flowers,
trees and animals live.
By the lake fairies dance and sing
with the magic of the stars
like diamonds in the night sky.
Fireflies flow through the air
with the full moon alight.
Fairy wings and fairy dust,
the magic spells of the night
fairy wings and fairy dust
flying in the light breeze of night.
Day break appears with the
dewy mists of valleys below,
magic spells of fairy land of delight.

Olive Irwin

THE WEIRD WITCH

I was sat beside the fire,
Reading the book of my desire,
Something touched me on my back,
I swung round; but all was black.

I crept upstairs towards my room,
Outside I found a witch's broom,
I peeped inside, and on the bed
There lay a witch who had no head!

She sprang up and grasped me tight,
Oh! What a scare! Oh! What a fright!
Suddenly I gave a scream,
Then I awoke; it was only a dream.

'It's those ghost stories I read last night,
They made me have that horrible fright.
But just think if it has been real,' I said,
'By now I'd be lying all cold - and *dead*!'

Ray Crutchlow

IT WASN'T ME, MISS

All through the years;
Keeps ringing in my ears . . .
'It wasn't me, Miss,
It wasn't me.'

'Pencils down; all stand!
Hold up your hands,
Palms facing me.
Now - let's see; 1,2,3,4,5,6,7,
Come to the front, No. 7.'

'What's this on your thumb?'
'I think it's chewing gum, Miss.'
'And where's the rest of it?'
Shout from the class:-
'It's in your hair, Miss.'

'Who put it there?'
A muffled cry from No. 7
'I did Miss, I'm sorry Miss.
Won't I go to Heaven then?'
'It depends on how good you are . . .
At washing hair!
First go and wash your hands!'
Stifled laughter from class.
Wry smile from teacher.

A-Betty Harrison

BEST FRIENDS

I have two very special friends,
They both live in my street.
We play together every night
Though we have to be discreet.

Harry, he's the eldest,
Is black and very handy.
Cyril has a gammy leg
And a weakness for cough candy.

I brought them home a week ago,
To meet my mum and dad,
But Mum just screamed and went all green
And Dad was just as bad!

I tried to say how good they were.
I said, 'Just keep your cool.'
Mum said, 'Get them out of here!'
And Dad jumped off his stool!

Dad said he would fetch a box,
To put my best friends in.
I said Dad could stroke one
Then they'd be friends with him.

Harry gave his biggest smile
And Cyril blew a kiss,
But Dad bashed down the rolling pin,
I prayed that he would miss!

My chums have got the message now,
They're feeling rather sad,
'Cos no-one loves a *tar-an-tu-la,*
Except for this brave lad!

Sue Hansard

SUPER!

In the comic books we're reading of heroes with super powers,
Faster than a bullet speeding - no wonder that they wow us,
As they leap across skyscrapers, or go soaring high above;
Having such exciting capers, and fighting because they're tough.
Answering to the names of Neutron Girl, Marvel man, Captain Fantastic
And Amazing Lad - the world is safe irrespective of how drastic
Things become, we shan't be glum. We'll sleep soundly in our beds,
Dreaming of the wars they've won, they're awesome, flying overhead.
With a secret identity they keep closely guarded,
They're the same as you and me, except when they discard it;
Then into a telephone booth they remove their suits
To emerge looking ultra-smooth, shod in shiny boots.
Dressed in yellow, red and blue, golden-silver, purple, green,
Costumes worn the whole year through, like every day's Halloween;
Wearing cloaks and masks, swearing to defend the human race
Against dastardly foes, daring villains and things from outer space.
Yes, we cheer our super heroes, while we read about their brawls;
How they run swifter than the wind blows, or how they crawl up walls.
Or maybe they can see through concrete, or themselves be seen through,
Men of iron who can't be beaten, strong as steel, brave and true.
Zap! A laser beam whizzes from a ray-gun straight toward
Panther Woman, but it misses, and she bounds overboard.
Pow! Astounding Man lands a punch, and Dr Dread is on the floor.
A-ha! Mr Mystery has a hunch he'll find who he's searching for.
Kaboom! Kid Dynamite takes flight, with The Lightning Bolt in tow.
Zoom-biff! Professor Midnight and Gorilla Boy come to blows.
Fisticuffs and mystic deeds, in the pages of the comics;
We witness this heroic breed in another fix,
From which they must escape to save us in the nick of time;
Super heroes in their capes and cowls, forever fighting crime.

Jonathan Goodwin

My Woolly Friend

My bear is called 'Woolly'
His coat is so soft
And though he can't tell me
He loves me a lot.

Each day, he is there
When I come through the door
If he could I am sure
He would hold out his paw!

He sits on the sofa
And watches the 'tele'
He laughs at the 'funnies'
He's ever so merry.

When it's time for his sleep
He flops on the floor
And I kiss him goodnight
And then, close the door.

Majorie H Smith

CAN YOU KEEP A SECRET?

Can you keep a secret?
I'm pretty sure you can!
It's all about the garden
And a little Goblin Man.
He works among the flowers
But he's very hard to see
Because he is so tiny
Not big, like you and me.

His job is never-ending
And he's busy all year through,
With mixing pots and brushes,
There's such a lot to do!
He has some willing helpers,
Three Pixies and two Elves,
Who hold the little bluebell pots
And mix the paint themselves.

Now when you see the raindrops
And the sun peeps through as well,
Here's the magic secret
You must promise not to tell!
The Goblin sends the Pixies
And the Elves away on high
To collect the brilliant colours
From the rainbow in the sky.

They paint each velvet petal
In orange, red or blue,
With indigo and violet
And heaps of yellow too;
And every leaf in shades of green
Completes the Master's plan,
Bringing beauty to your garden
From the little Goblin Man.

Pat Watson

THE LITTLE PUFF

There was a railway engine
Called, 'The Little Puff',
Who rolled all day on railway tracks
Made of frozen fluff.

His wheels were ginger biscuits,
And his pipes were spaghetti lines;
His whistle cost a penny,
And he always ran on time!

The grill at front was toasted bread,
His windows were but wafers,
And the chimney was a few old sticks
Covered with brown paper.

Passenger people stood and smiled
Whenever he took mail,
At the funniest-looking engine
In the whole of British Rail!

A R Hawthorn

TICK TACK TAVEY

Tick Tack Tavey the rebel clock
Ticked quite loudly but would not tock
Tick tock, tick tock the other clocks sang
As Pepo the clockmaker's hammer rang
Happily making clocks to sell
Pepo was baffled by Tavey's rebel
Why won't you tick and tock like the others?
Is there something missing, behave like your brothers!
But Tavey ignored poor Pepo's pleas
He tick tacked away as if to tease
A clock such as you no one will buy
The other clocks agreed with a sigh
This made Tavey's plan complete
The shop was his home so clean and neat
He loved Pepo and planned to stay
Happily tick and tacking away
As time passed by Pepo and he
Lived happily ever after as all could see.

Catherine Hislop

UNCLE HORACE

Uncle Horace is rather old now,
And he looks a little battered.
One eye has gone, an arm hangs loose,
And his fur is rather tattered.

He's been all round the countryside
On the back seat of many a car.
He's been on trains and boats and planes,
Uncle Horace has travelled far.

The family have known him now,
For many a long year.
He's been a friend to all the kids,
One they all hold dear.

No-one knows for sure of course,
Just how old he might be.
And Uncle Horace will never tell,
Perhaps he's ninety-three!

One thing's for sure, at bedtime,
When it's time to sleep and rest.
There's no one better to lay beside,
Uncle Horace is the best!

It's said that many years ago,
He was brought home from a fair.
And he's been here ever since you know,
That dear old Teddy Bear.

Brian L Porter

LITTLE BLACKIE

Within my weekends,
away from school,
I would dance through fields,
nearby - so cool,
until one day - out of the blue,
a puppy appeared,
as black as a shoe.

Where did you descend from,
my little black lamb?
You must be lost - surely,
my name is Sam,
we danced and played,
for many long hours,
myself and little Blackie,
jumping over the flowers.

Each weekend I spent,
playing among the grass,
little Blackie appeared,
so bold as brass,
I'll call you Blackie,
for you're so divine,
he gave a glad woof,
so now he is mine.

Steve Kettlewell

BEAR

He sat on his bottom
Looking old, tattered and torn,
Straw poking through his stitches,
His fur bald in places
Like a retired old gentleman.
His early years of being pampered,
Bounced downstairs
From which ever limb,
Forced to eat jelly and ice cream,
Sharing those early wet patches,
Being left in the garden when it rained,
Hung from the washing line by the ears.
Now those years are over
Sitting on the shelf to age,
Propping up a book or two.
A still much loved bear.
What a life
Being a bear.

Ted Pyman

IN FRONT OF THE LOOKING GLASS

'This must be the Dance of Fire',
Thinks Alice, seeing figures in the flames,
As she sits by the fireplace, tightly curled
In the furthest corner of her favourite chair,
And weeps for her lost world, her fantasy world.

Stan Downing

ALIEN ENCOUNTER

Mark, my mate, has some funny ideas.
Today he said, 'You know Barney McGregor?'
'Yes . . .'
'Well we all know he's a clever beggar,
Good at everything - a real genius he is.
But I think there's more to it than that,
And if I'm wrong I'll eat my hat.
Take a close look at him - it's not a human you're seeing,
I'm sure McGregor's an Alien Being.'
I swallowed hard, but let him continue,
When Mark's in full flow that's the only thing to do.
'One day his skin will crack and peel
Like an egg shell splitting, or splintering wood,
And oozing out will come luminous blood.
His head will slide back, underneath to reveal
A purple brain, pulsing like a jelly-fish.
From his nose thin tentacles black as liquorice
Will grow. Both eyes will gradually expand,
And giant green scabs will grow on all six hands . . .'
Just then Barney came sauntering into view.
Quite what he was up to we didn't understand,
He was holding a litter picker in his hand.
He grinned when he saw us. 'Hi there you two!
I'm searching for foil - aluminium you know.
When I've filled my bag here, it's to the bank I go.
Recycling bank that is - you know where I mean?
I try my hardest these days to be really green.'

As he picked his way further down the road,
Mark watched him closely then whispered to me,

'Did you hear what he said, Jay? Really weird . . .
He'll start to turn any day now - just you see.'

Trevor Cattell

Football Is A Funny Old Game

Football is a funny old game,
Score a goal and the fans are never the same.
As they all chant and roar,
Asking for more.
As they support their favourite team,
Nothing is what it seems,
The players run around the football pitch like new-born foals,
All because they have scored a few goals.
When all they do is kick a ball around,
From one end of the football ground.
Trying to hit the net,
And it is not even half time yet.
The fans want their team to win,
As if they don't, it is like a sin.
Football is a funny old game,
Watch your team win and you'll never be the same.
As the fans will be on cloud nine,
When the match has finished at full time.

Tina Rooney

WHAT'S IT CALLED?

Once there was a man who lived beside the sea,
He had a little house and was happy as could be,
But he forgot a lot - he grew worse every day
And when he went around the town you would hear him say:-

Do you remember what's-is-name, the man with the thingummy jig?
I don't recall his father at all, but his mother wore a wig,
When he married you-know-who or was her name Elaine?
They moved away to I-don't-know-where and were never seen again.

As the time passed by his memory grew worse,
Eventually he died and they buried him - of course,
As they left the churchyard where the old man lay
His friends were quite surprised when they thought they heard him say:-

I hope I'm going to you-know-where and not to whatever-it's-called,
I think I've led a good life, but St Peter may be appalled,
Once I get my you-know-what I think I'll learn to sing,
I suppose I'll have to practise a lot on whatever-you-call-the-thing.

George Main

BUBBLES

Bubbles bright as baby's eyes,
Bouncing sailing through blue skies,
The sun all dressed in gold above,
Dancing sunbeam dreams of love,
Now Mr Rain has gone away,
This is a day just made for play,
All pretty rainbow colours see;
The best of times for you and me.

Nigel David Evans

UNDERNEATH THE STAIRS

Underneath the stairs
There lives a dragon,
With fiery breath and
A mighty roar,
This dragon though
He seemed fierce
Was as friendly
As you and me,
His big flapping wings
Disturbed not even a mouse,
Yet he lived in our house,
He just appeared one day,
At night his noisy snore
Keeps everyone awake,
He never comes out
Except at the dead of night,
When we have eventually
Gone to sleep,
He has the most amazing
Adventures to tell,
Of knights doing battle
And they did chase him so,
So if you come to our
House and look under the stairs,
Don't get a fright at the sight of the
Dragon living there.

Penny Wright

THE WITCH

She was dressed in black from head to toe
and her eyes I swear did glower,
petrified with fright at her presence there
beneath the bedclothes I did cower.

What do you want? I finally spoke
cringing in my cosy bed,
from her open mouth poured pungent smoke
and I waited for her answer with dread.

Not a sound came from the tall, dark witch
she just stood at my bedroom door,
the sight of her made me shake and twitch
for I had never seen her likeness before.

Suddenly the door opened wide, my mother
stood framed in light,
I could not pretend to be asleep I was so filled
with delight.

It was my dressing gown on the door,
the colour flaming red,
it was my dressing gown in the dark
which has filled me with fearful dread.

Grace Whyte

SCAMP

This is the story of a dog called Scamp,
who would not go walkies in the damp
when his mum said how do you do
he said be quiet, I'm having my chew.
Cor! I don't know which biscuit to choose
I think I'll lay on me beanbag and have a snooze,
but before I lay down with a plop
I'm going to scrounge a chocolate drop.

John Clarke

My Clock

I have a pretty little clock,
Which works all night and day,
It tells me when to go to school,
And when it's time to play,
It tells me when to go to bed,
And when it's time to rise,
So, though it never says a word,
It must be very wise.

Matthew L Burns

DANNY SINGS

One thing all corgis are good at
Is singing both serious and pop
And Danny was no exception
In the choir he was the tops
Then like Aled Jones before him
His prowess began to be known
And soon he was noticed by others
Who wanted to make him a dog of renown
The difficulty was to choose whether
Glyndebourne or Glastonbury
All Danny enjoyed was the music
No matter which style it should be
In the end he went to the Festival
And made a hit instantly
He was even invited to sing
In a programme for Welsh BBC
So he stayed with them for a series
'Til one day an entrepreneur
Approached him with the suggestion
That he should take him on tour
A very excited young singer
Who welcomed the future in store
Danny packed his bags and his music
Set off on his travels once more.

Barbara Williams

I Hate

O yuck, O smuck,
It's clear to me
I hate everything and everyone
That is dear to me.

Can't do this
Don't do that
Keep on your
Strangle that poor cat.

I like licking my fingers, picking my nose
Flicking my peas
Pulling off scabs
When I graze my knees

I like climbing trees
Playing in mud
Crunching snails
Or eating a grub

I like everything
Grown ups hate
Better go nearly
Tea time I hate to be late.

Ann Weavers

THE MILK COW

I am a milk cow
I love to chew the cud,
I eat all the green grass,
Because it does me good,
I have a swishy tail,
My back's as pure as silk,
When I go in the barn at night,
I give the farmer lots of milk . . .

G Bannister

A Knight's Tale

Ronaldo, that sweet 'Gentil' Knight, rode forth,
Spurred, fully armoured head to toe was he,
With bannered lance, and his two-handed sword
And some fair ladies' favours, flown to see.

Seated on a small ass beside him, rode
His page, a dour tall man from Burgundy,
His over-long thin legs were lifted so
To clear the clods they rode upon, so free.
But while the Knight was hale, well-fed and sleek
Warmly enrobed in comfort sat his horse,
The Page did shiver, and his visage bleak
Had nose from which continued drips had course,
No cheerful serf or willing servant he,
Unpaid, ill-fed, and dressed in raggy clothes,
Each day he felt ill-used by this Grandee!

The maid they found imprisoned to that post
Where brave Ronaldo slew that fiery beast,
Claimed with kisses, the maiden for his own!
Then Page said, 'Oy Mate! What's in this for me?
For many a bad day I've scrimped and groaned
About the grub, and lack of wage or fee!
So there, while you two snog, I'll swiftly go,
Take your horse and robe, and flog them off with glee!

You'll find that here's a very frosty zone
While rescued Maid will in a taxi leave.
Then you in your pin-pointed visor moan
Of hindered sight, and minus trusty steed,
Will rust and stagger, clank your way to home,
'Gentil Knight!' Forsooth! So be wise, take heed,
In future, pay your Page his daily 'dough'!

Ron Hammond

There's A Hole In Your Hair

There's a hole in your hair Grandpa,
I saw it last night,
When you bent down to kiss me,
And Mary, goodnight.
But never mind Grandpa;
You're still as fit as can be.
You can still run, and jump,
Like all my friends and me.

And I'll tell you what Grandpa,
I'll get some of mummy's grey wool
And patch up that hole,
Until it's quite full.

Y Blake

Lottery

There was an old man from Kerry,
Who was always so jolly and merry,
Always so calm and cool,
'Til he stepped in a lump of dog's poo,
His shoe it was covered in muck,
Maybe it would bring him some luck,
He purchased a lottery ticket,
Slipped and he fell in a thicket,
His smile it was gradually waning,
Next thing it was bloomin' well raining,
With a coin he scratched and he scratched,
Three symbols emerged and they matched,
He couldn't believe he had won,
A holiday out in the sun,
Next time that you see a dog's poo,
Step in it - this could be you!

W Curran

BENJY THE BEAR

I once had a teddy called Benjy the bear,
He had buttons for eyes,
And brown shaggy hair.
Wherever I went,
He'd ask to come too!
When I went to school,
When I sat on the loo!
But what no one did see, was when we were alone,
we went on adventures, in the great unknown!
A dragon had kept prisoner a beautiful princess,
She was trapped in a cage,
And in awful distress!
Benjy the bear, he was so brave,
He fought with that dragon,
And so gracefully did save,
The beautiful princess, who gave him a sword,
And asked him quite kindly would he be a lord?
But poor Benjy the bear had to refuse,
Because he was so frightened more stuffing he'd lose!
So he decided to come home with me instead,
And together we snuggled up in our nice comfy bed!

Rachel Harrison

TICK-TOCK, BEDROOM CLOCK

Tick-tock,
Bedroom clock
Waken me on a day
Of pealing bells
And magic spells
And laughter at all that I say.

If I cry help the tears to dry
And my day will be full of you.

Tick-tock,
Bedroom clock
Till sleep quietens you,
Faces and places
May leave their traces
But embraces make it all true.

Take the time to tickle me pink
And I'll give all my love to you.

Pip Hill

THE SILLIEST FAIRY TALE

When Jack went up the beanstalk
He took a leg of pork
A sack of new potatoes
And a nice clean knife and fork
As he didn't know what to expect
When he reached the top
Thought there may not be any water
So he took a bottle of pop
Now when he was almost half way up
He met - coming down
With a monkey on his shoulder
A funny circus clown
Who said to him politely
I think you should be aware
That you will need an overcoat
For its very cold up there
He thanked the clown most kindly
Thinking it's too late to turn back now
So he carried on right to the top
Now this was in the summertime
When it was very dry and hot
And the bean stalk needed watering
But Jack's mother alas forgot
So it just withered and died
To Jack's mum's great despair
Who just sat down and cried
For Jack's still stuck up there
So go and get some bean seeds
And plant them in a row
Give them lots of water
So that they quickly grow

Do this every single day
Until they're fully grown
For that is now the only way
To help get poor Jack down.

H H Steventon

THE WOODS WITH ROBIN

I believed in Robin Hood
Yes that man in green,
I would have loved to have
Worn 'Lincoln green' -
And to have become Robin's queen -
Well 'Maid Marion' was his true love
I could have been like her in a way,
Around the woods, I could have sung
Many times each day.
Fryer Tuck, he loved his food
That's why he was big and round,
But Little John
He should have looked after
Robin - more,
As they went off together
To rob the rich to give unto the poor.
For Little John was a big man
His arrows he could aim -
He could knock Alan Adale out cold,
If any argument got involved,
But Robin my man in green
You loved the down and outs,
What fun I could have had
In the woods with you in your day,
For us two together we would
Have made the rich to pay.

Marion Staddon

AT THE TEA PARTY WITH ALICE

Stare stare
the March hare
hare off, hairy legs
chary legs
here's the Mad Hatter
chatterbox
chatter teeth
biting holes in teacups
pass the sugar
pass the milk-jug
to jug the hare

Elaine Harris

SNOW MARTYR

At first it seemed we ran
as melting snow together.
So must we now in parting
dribble into drains?

Must love wear thin on postcards?
or empty down the tunnelled mind
of phone calls?

Could we not form a lake, a lap of love,
a spring, a well to fill each tap?
Whose motions in our life could bring
not petty impulses
but crackerjacks that leap for fun?

But now it seems love dies.
Its day is done.

George Pearson

Last Word

My conker's bigger than your conker,
My marble's faster than yours.
My football's a better bouncer,
My skipping rope's longer than yours.

My daddy's bigger than your daddy,
My mummy's prettier than yours.
My sister's a better dancer,
My brother's much stronger than yours.

My eyes aren't as watchful as your eyes,
My reflexes slower than yours.
My legs are all wobbly now, but . . .
My eye will be blacker than yours.

Liz Sinclair

MY KIDS

My kids
Good kids
Kind kids
Lovely kids

Not other people's kids
My kids
Loving giving - do no wrong
My kids

Tall kids, short kids
Fat kids, thin kids
Yellow, brown and white kids
Nice kids

What's for tea? Mum - kids
Jelly for my tum - kids
Running round the block - kids
Happy kids

Where's the aftershave - Dad
Can I have the car - Dad
Mum - this is Rachel
Grown up kids

Can you babysit Mum?
Come to us for tea Mum
Thanks for being Mum, Mum
No longer little kids but forever
My kids

Patricia Richards

MY GIRL

Danielle is bright and bubbly,
Also soft and cuddly.
She doesn't stop talking,
Only when she takes the dog a walking.
With her long dark hair and hazel eyes,
She laughs a lot, but cries when she says her goodbyes.
Her talking drives me round the twist,
But I wouldn't be without her, I love her to bits!
In her absence the deathly silence creeps upon me,
I do not like it, upon her return I smile with glee,
And am delighted to see my daughter,
Once more who I wouldn't alter.

Pamela Butcher

KIDZ

Kids today
Oh what can I say
No respect in what we say
Let's hope they hear a word or two
And maybe we'll get through
The moods and chill out attitude
We hold our breath and sigh a sigh
Until the years go rolling by
But saying this you must agree
Kids today are here to stay

Margaret Grayson

EVEN BIGGER KIDS!

Kids on the corner,
Kids on the street,
Kids in the house, getting under my feet.
'Where's my tea?'
'I'm watching that telly'
'Where's my socks?' - 'Yes those are smelly!'
'Have you seen my shirt or my football kit?'
'Are these my shorts, they don't seem to fit'

Yes kids of today are so sad,
But I'm just talking about . . .
Their *dad!*

Paula McKee

My Child Dream

I look back now, what do I see?
A sweet little girl at the age of three.
She is standing there smiling, blonde and tall,
Very proud, holding tight a football.

As she grew older, her friends were boys,
With them she could play football, not play with toys.
She became equal to them as she became older,
No boy could beat her, she became bolder.

Kel was chosen for Everton, at the age of nine,
Two years she spent on the defensive line.
From there to Burnley, where she shone,
A strong centre forward, second to none.

To see my daughter, with her long blonde hair,
Heart full of love and skin so fair.
You could never imagine how strong she could be,
With a football at her feet, I wish you could see.

Kellie's at the Centre of Excellence, working hard,
For the day when England give her the call.
That day I will be there, standing proud,
Tears in my eyes, shouting out loud.

This is for the precious daughter whom I love so much
Who has fought many obstacles, to play the game she loves.

Jenny Leyland

WHAT TO WEAR

Should I wear my green skirt?
No, the colour's too bright - Zina will make fun of me.

Shall I wear my grey top?
No, it's way out of style - Kirsty will laugh.

Shall I wear my black trousers?
No, you can see the mend - Sandra from 9H will spot it.

Shall I wear my pink scarf?
No, I wore it last week - Aisha will notice.

What to wear?
What to wear?
What to wear?

Dressing for school is such a pain.
Can't wear this, can't wear that.

Sometimes, I wish teachers had a uniform too.

Lynn Schrale

CHILDREN

C ute
H appy
I nnocent
L oving
D emanding
R emarkable
E njoyable
N oisy

Patricia McGuigan

GIVEN AWAY

Where were you on parents' night?
Duty day again
And when the school bazaar was held
Why were you away?
Report due in I expect and
I'm a social worker's kid

When I read my play to you
Why were you asleep?
And when the field trip returned home
Why was I the last?
Conference on, ran over and
I'm just a social worker's kid

The tea is late
The house a mess
But we can wait
And we can guess
When you'll be back

Where were you on Saturday?
Another report?
And when I went to bed that night,
You were writing still
I read myself to sleep and said
I'm a social worker's kid

When I'm asked what will I do?
I will tell them all
Not a social worker, never that -
To make my children feel
Other kids counted more and my time
Could be given away.

Jessica Bartlett

THE BIG KIDS

My teacher is very boring
At football he's no good at scoring
I cannot understand his writing
But he always stops us from fighting
We're not allowed to mess about
Or we get sent out.

My dad loves the teletext
And what will he think of next
He always falls to sleep
But he does it in a big heap
He likes to watch football
And he hates basketball.

My mum helps us with our work
When I get stuck my brother has to smirk
My mum talks to the wall
But we don't care at all
She helps me get ready for football
And she says 'I'm getting tall.'

Liam Bates

CHAMELEON

One minute she is happy
A whirlwind in the house
The next she's in her bedroom
As quiet as a mouse.

Today she is a hippy
Bright clothes, long flowing hair
The next she will be daring
To make the people stare.

My daughter can be helpful
Polite and nice to know
But she can also be a nightmare
Moody, when she's low.

A student to be proud of
Working hard at school
but when the wind changes
She enjoys acting out the fool.

My daughter is a complex child
She changes every day
But I would not have her different
Not in any single way.

Jennie Atkinson

TODAY'S YOUTH

They all sit on the bench
In the middle of the town
Calling obscene things to others
And pushing each other down

They're swearing and they're fighting
Throwing stones at people's cars
Getting drunk and taking drugs
So they start seeing stars

So this is the younger generation
It makes me shake and shudder
You see it really frightens me
Because I am a mother.

Julie Grinney

IT

My kids are streaks ahead of me
It hertz I have to say.
Working at our computer
It's easy Mam they say

We'll monitor what you do Mam
You'll tower above us we know
But I am not sure I can
Why do I need to look in a window

It Bytes that I'm so ignorant
When I want to be so cool
But I have no idea
What is a proofing tool?

If my memory serves me right
They tell me there's a mouse
Maybe the Ram will eat it
I don't want mice in the house

They say they have a floppy disc
I have some cream for that
Just pull up your shirt my pet
And lay face down on the mat

I am going to try very hard though
With the kids help I am not going to fail
Into the chat rooms I'll go
And people will send me e-mail

Valerie Ramsey

JAMES, 13, SO FAR

It all went so fast . . .

Baa baa black sheep, have you any wool?

It's three o'clock in the morning
I want to sleep
Baby wants to eat
It's so unfair,
He always wins

Yes sir, yes sir, three bags full

It's half past three in the morning
I look at him
Is this a dream?
He smiles at me!

One for the master, one for the dame

It's Christmas Day
The house is merry
Noise and food
Drinks and parcels
Everywhere
And then silence
The house is still . . .
The little boy is walking!

One for the little boy that lives down the lane

It's dinner time
I want to eat
I want to clear up
I want to rest

A deep voice asks:
'Mum, what is communism?'
The washing up will have to wait . . .
He always wins

D Slade

BIG KIDS ON LITTLE KIDS

I was afraid of the world when I was a child,
Disorder, mistrust and everything wild.
The cars on the road and the kids at the park.
Shadows on walls that crept in with the dark.
Invisible monsters that no one could see,
Lay under my bed to jump out on me.
Afraid to tell the truth but afraid to lie.
Not wanting to say - just wanting to cry.
But as you get older the more that you know
That life's not so scary as you continue to grow.
There aren't any monsters waiting to call,
And the shadows - reflections that dance on the wall.
The kids on the park, have kids of their own,
And the car you were afraid of is outside your home . . .
So try to be happy - don't wish life away,
You're not a child long - you'll be grown up one day.

Karen Cormick

BIG KIDS ON KIDS

Kids - what are they good for
    absolutely everything.

Kids - the good the bad and the ugly -
    all are wonderful in the eyes of Mother.

Kids - they bring you joy they bring you pain,
    but more often they bring you dirty washing.

Kids - they come in all shapes and sizes
    and often with holes in their trousers.

Kids - something in the way he smiles
    affects me like no other.

Kids - the world over whatever their creed
    whatever their colour are sent to make life what it is
    without them we would all be the weakest link -
                                Goodbye.

Greta Boyd

SWIFTLY GO THE YEARS

When you were one, I had such fun,
Watching you flourish and grow.
I thought I'd be a perfect Mum,
And learn all there was to know.
By the time that you were four years old -
You wouldn't do a thing you were told.
When you were six, you played such tricks,
Life was a constant battle of wits.
When you were eight, you were such a brat,
You wouldn't eat this - wouldn't wear that,
By the age of ten, we were friends again,
And you were such a smarty.
Always giggling, full of fun, asked to every party.
I tried to teach you right from wrong -
Hoped you would grow up honest and strong.
I saw you through your teenage years,
Helped to allay your worries and fears.
I loved your presence about the place,
But tried to give you your own space.
And now that you have flown the nest,
I know that I was truly blessed
To have a daughter just like you,
My dearest friend, my whole life through.

Maureen Smith

WELL ROUNDED CITIZENS

Prayed my children's lives would be different to mine,
Spent hours playing with them, having quality time.
Took them on journeys to places of interest,
On holidays went to the seaside, liked this best.

Tried to impress the need of good education,
Jobs offered to one with great qualification.
But of course, they all rebelled and went their own way,
At last, years later, believed what I used to say.

Without grades needed, they find it hard to survive,
Though they became well rounded citizens aged five.

S Mullinger

THE CHILDREN

I heard the voices again
Children's voices subdued sometimes
Sometimes giggling
As if they were hiding from one another.

Then calling to one another
'Where are you?'
'I can't find you!'
'Come out wherever you are.'

The room was full of sunshine
Dust floating on the beams of light
As the wood in the old house
Settled in the warm sun.

I hear them running downstairs
And I step into the hall
'Who are you?' I ask
And there is silence.

I can feel their presence
As though they watch me.
Then I hear their voices again
Giggling and laughing together.

As they run back upstairs
Their footsteps echoing
In the quiet house
Then all is still again.

The past is ever with us
As is the future
And one is enfolded in the other
Time is but a measure.

The happiness of the boys
Enfolds me
Are they in a time warp
Or just shadows that come and go?

I will never know
Because I have to move on
To create my own impressions
Or shadows to leave behind.

J Wills

LITTLE CHILDREN

Bless,
The little children,
Who walk,
Upon this ground.

Bless,
The little children,
Who from Heaven,
Do look down.

Bless,
The little children,
For so precious,
Are they.

Bless,
The little children,
As they softly,
Laugh,
And play.

D Begley

GROWING

The night my son was born I felt like a king
Such a beautiful innocent little thing
Dirty face and clothes and smelly nappy
But when he smiled we were so happy

I remember the day he took his first step
We were over the moon and almost wept
And as for the day he said his first word
A voice more like an angel has never been heard

Then his first day at the local school
In his little uniform he looked so cool
The years went by he grew big and strong
And with my help he learned right from wrong

Although he likes his music loud
He never ceases to make me proud
And if he sees a girl he thinks is nice
Then he comes to me for my advice

But all too soon he will leave our home
And set out to find a life of his own
Even then I still can't complain
A million memories will remain

Paul O'Boyle

CAPPED INNOCENCE

Shining hairless young heads.
Not shed by razor's edge
but 'Chemotherapy,'
mirror 'Cancer's' grasping search.

You glisten atop sad eyes
without their glint of youth.
Contrasted against taut skin,
paled, aged as parchment.

Too young to be guilty,
of perpetrated sin.
No quisling offence here,
prompts cropping of their heads.

Condemned without fair trial
to suffer vicious growth.
Enduring treatment's torments
perchance to reach your panacea.

Leslie Fine

CHILDHOOD DREAMS

You think rainbow clouds are pink
as with your hands swizzing around in the sink
as white bubbles blowing around on the floor
as you're not a toddler anymore.

Sitting there working out all the maths homework
What's it all about?

You take a cloth to help me out
All the dusting just us three
While all the TV programmes shout alone
You press the button to drown out the sound.

I can't believe how grown you want to be
When all I can remember
Is the baby you used to be.

A J Renyard

ANCHOR BOOKS
SUBMISSIONS INVITED
SOMETHING FOR EVERYONE

ANCHOR BOOKS GEN - Any subject, light-hearted clean fun, nothing unprintable please.

THE OPPOSITE SEX - Have your say on the opposite gender. Do they drive you mad or can we co-exist in harmony?

THE NATURAL WORLD - Are we destroying the world around us? What should we do to preserve the beauty and the future of our planet - you decide!

All poems no longer than 30 lines.
Always welcome! No fee!
Plus cash prizes to be won!

Mark your envelope (eg *The Natural World*)
And send to:
Anchor Books
Remus House, Coltsfoot Drive
Peterborough, PE2 9JX

OVER £10,000 IN POETRY PRIZES TO BE WON!

Send an SAE for details on our New Year 2002 competition!